Colorado

A Buddy Book
by
Julie Murray

ABDO
Publishing Company

VISIT US AT

www.abdopub.com

Published by ABDO Publishing Company, 4940 Viking Drive, Edina, Minnesota 55435.

Printed in the United States.

Edited by: Sarah Tieck
Contributing Editor: Michael P. Goecke
Graphic Design: Deb Coldiron, Maria Hosley
Image Research: Sarah Tieck
Photographs: clipart.com, Creatas, EyeWire, Getty Images, One Mile Up, PhotoDisc, Photos.com

Library of Congress Cataloging-in-Publication Data

Murray, Julie, 1969-
   Colorado / Julie Murray.
      p. cm. — (The United States)
   Includes bibliographical references and index.
   ISBN 1-59197-665-0
      1. Colorado—Juvenile literature. I. Title.

F776.3.M87 2005
978.8—dc22

                                        2004047746

Table Of Contents

A Snapshot Of Colorado

Colorado is a beautiful state. It is known for its scenic land and wildlife. When people think of Colorado, they think of mountains, gorges, and rivers.

Colorado got its name from Spanish explorers in the 1600s. They named the Colorado River. Colorado is a Spanish word. It means "colored red." This came from the red canyons around the river.

There are 50 states in the United States. Every state is different. Every state has an official state nickname. Colorado is called the "Centennial State." This is because Colorado became a state in 1876. The 100-year anniversary of the Declaration of Independence was in 1876.

Red cliffs surround the Colorado River. They inspired its name.

Colorado has 104,100 square miles (269,618 sq km) of land. It is the eighth-largest state in the United States. The United States government owns about a third of this land. There are 4,301,261 people who call Colorado home.

Millions of people live in Colorado.

Where Is Colorado?

There are four parts of the United States. Each part is called a region. Each region is in a different area of the country. The United States Census Bureau says the four regions are the Northeast, the South, the Midwest, and the West.

The state of Colorado is located in the West region of the United States. The weather in Colorado is cool. There is snow in some parts of the mountains all year long.

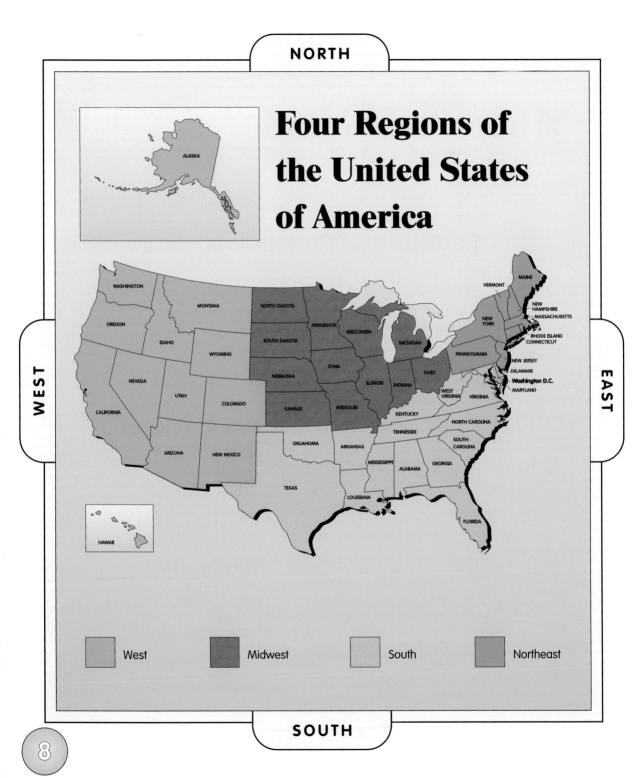

ALASKA

Four Regions of the United States of America

WASHINGTON
MONTANA
NORTH DAKOTA
MINNESOTA
VERMONT
MAINE
OREGON
IDAHO
WYOMING
SOUTH DAKOTA
WISCONSIN
MICHIGAN
NEW YORK
NEW HAMPSHIRE
MASSACHUSETTS
RHODE ISLAND
CONNECTICUT
NEVADA
UTAH
COLORADO
NEBRASKA
IOWA
ILLINOIS
INDIANA
OHIO
PENNSYLVANIA
NEW JERSEY
DELAWARE
CALIFORNIA
KANSAS
MISSOURI
WEST VIRGINIA
VIRGINIA
Washington D.C.
MARYLAND
ARIZONA
NEW MEXICO
OKLAHOMA
ARKANSAS
KENTUCKY
TENNESSEE
NORTH CAROLINA
SOUTH CAROLINA
TEXAS
MISSISSIPPI
ALABAMA
GEORGIA
LOUISIANA
FLORIDA

HAWAII

West   Midwest   South   Northeast

Colorado is bordered by seven different states. Wyoming borders Colorado to the north. Nebraska lies on the northeast corner of the state. Kansas is located to the east. Oklahoma and New Mexico lie to the south and Utah is to the west. Arizona touches the southwest corner of the state.

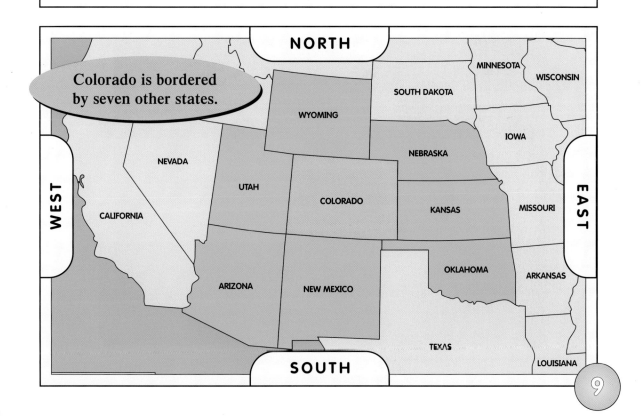

Colorado is bordered by seven other states.

Colorado

State abbreviation: CO

State nickname: The Centennial State

State capital: Denver

State motto: Nil sine numine (Latin for "Nothing without providence")

Statehood: August 1, 1876, 38th state

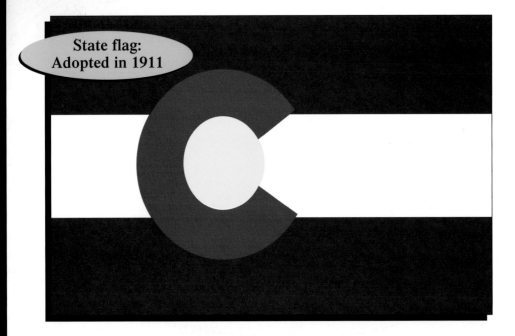

State flag:
Adopted in 1911

Population: 4,301,261, ranks 24th

Land area: 104,100 square miles (269,618 sq km), ranks 8th

State tree: Colorado blue spruce

State song: "Where the Columbines Grow"

State government: Three branches: legislative, executive, and judicial

Average July temperature: 74°F (23°C)

Average January temperature: 28°F (-2°C)

State flower: White and Lavender Columbine

State bird: Lark Bunting

State animal: Rocky Mountain Bighorn Sheep

Cities And The Capital

Denver is the capital of Colorado. It is also its largest city, with 554,636 residents. Denver is at the base of the Rocky Mountains. It is called "The Mile High City." That is because the stairway on the west side of the capitol building reaches 5,280 feet (1,609 m) above sea level. That is the same as one mile.

The United States Mint is in Denver. The Denver Mint makes United States coins. Some common United States coins are quarters, dimes, nickels, and pennies. Look at a coin. If the letter "D" is stamped on it, it was made in Denver.

Downtown Denver has many skyscrapers.

A view of the Capitol building in Denver.

Colorado Springs is in the Rocky Mountains. It is the second-largest city in Colorado. It is located south of Denver. Colorado Springs is known for being sunny. The city averages 300 sunny days each year.

The United States Air Force Academy is located near Colorado Springs. This is where people train for jobs in the United States Air Force. Many tourists also come here.

Colorado has many scenic areas.

Famous Citizens

M. Scott Carpenter (1925–)

M. Scott Carpenter was born in Boulder. He was one of the first United States astronauts. He was the second American to orbit the earth in a spaceship. In 1962, Carpenter orbited Earth three times in *Aurora 7*. Scott Carpenter also did deep-sea research. In 1965, he did experiments on the ocean floor.

M. Scott Carpenter

Famous Citizens

Lon Chaney (1883–1930)

Lon Chaney was born in Colorado Springs in 1883. He was an actor. He was called the "Man of a Thousand Faces." He starred in many classic horror movies. He used lots of make-up for his movie roles. This helped his characters look more real. One of his films was *The Phantom of the Opera*. He played The Phantom in the 1925 silent version.

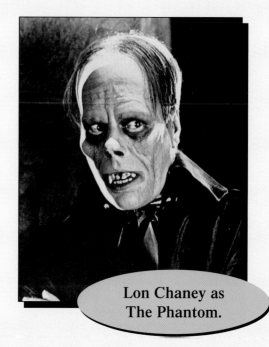

Lon Chaney as The Phantom.

The Rocky Mountains

Much of the land in Colorado is made up of the Rocky Mountains. The Rocky Mountains run through the center of the state. The Rocky Mountains is the largest mountain chain in North America. They stretch 3,000 miles (4,828 km) through the United States and Canada. They are 350 miles (563 km) wide in some places.

There are 55 mountain peaks over 14,000 feet (4,267 m) high in Colorado. The tallest mountain peak in Colorado is Mount Elbert. It is 14,433 feet (4,399 m) high.

This lake is in the Rocky Mountains.

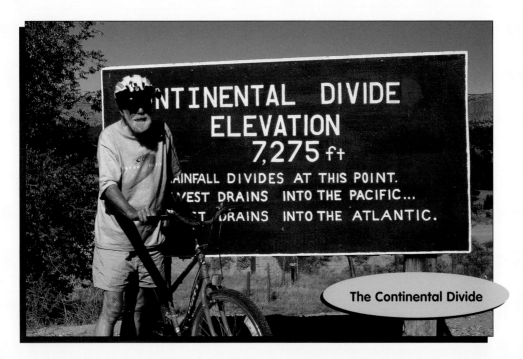

The Continental Divide

Along the top ridge of the Rocky Mountains runs the Continental Divide. There is the eastern slope and the western slope. Rivers on the western slope flow west into the Pacific Ocean. Rivers on the eastern slope flow east into the Atlantic Ocean.

Rocky Mountain National Park is one of Colorado's most famous spots. The park covers 265,828 acres (107,577 hectares) of land. Visitors come here to see views of the mountains. Also, people hike, bike, fish, and ride horses in the park. Many animals live in the park. Bighorn sheep, mountain goats, elk, and bears roam free.

Mesa Verde National Park

   Mesa Verde National Park is a plateau. Mesa Verde is Spanish for "green table." More than 400,000 people visit this national park each year.

   The Anasazi Cliff Dwellings are in Mesa Verde National Park. People go there to learn about the Anasazi Indians. The Anasazi lived there from 600 B.C. to A.D. 1300. The Anasazi are known for making baskets.

Cliff Palace

They are also known for living in cliff dwellings about 800 years ago. The cliff dwellings were built into the side of the plateau or canyon walls. Many have several levels and rooms. The largest one is Cliff Palace. It is four stories tall with more than 200 rooms.

National Monuments

Dinosaur National Monument has many dinosaur fossils. One exhibit shows 1,500 fossils. There is even a town near Dinosaur National Monument called Dinosaur. Some of the streets in the town are named after dinosaurs.

There are many dinosaur fossils in museums.

Great Sand Dunes National Monument has the tallest sand dunes found in North America. The dunes rise up more than 700 feet (213 m). In 2004, Great Sand Dunes National Monument officially became Great Sand Dunes National Park.

The landscape of Great Sand Dunes National Park.

The Great Sand Dunes were created from the erosion of nearby mountains. This happened over thousands of years. The sand dunes still change every day. The wind and rain shape them.

Colorado

1600s: Spanish explorers are the first Europeans in Colorado. They name the Colorado River. Colorado means "colored red."

1706: Juan de Ulibarri claims Colorado for Spain.

1806: Zebulon Pike discovers Pikes Peak in the Rocky Mountains.

A view of Pikes Peak.

1858: Gold is discovered at Dry Creek, near what is now Denver.

1861: The Colorado Territory is created.

1867: Denver is named the seat of government of the Colorado Territory.

1869: The world's first rodeo takes place on July 4 in Deer Trail.

1876: Colorado becomes the 38th state on August 1.

1893: Colorado votes as a state to allow women to vote.

1893: Katherine Lee Bates writes "America the Beautiful." She was inspired by the view from the top of Pikes Peak.

1906: The United States Mint in Denver makes its first coins.

1915: President Woodrow Wilson creates Rocky Mountain National Park.

1925: Royal Gorge Bridge is built. This is the highest suspension bridge in the world. The Arkansas River is 1,053 feet (321 m) below the bridge.

1958: The United States Air Force Academy opens in August.

1997–1998: The Denver Broncos win two Super Bowls in a row.

Cities in Colorado

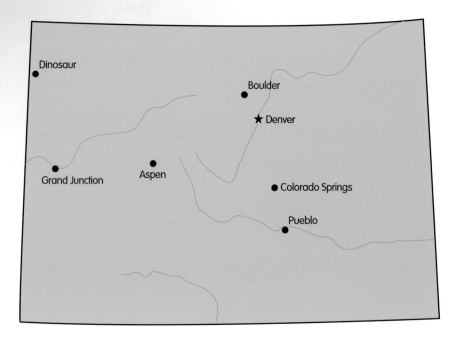

Important Words

capital a city where government leaders meet.

centennial 100-year anniversary.

Continental Divide a place on the top ridge of the Rocky Mountains that divide North America. Some rivers flow into the Pacific Ocean and some flow into the Atlantic Ocean.

Declaration of Independence a very important paper of American history. It explains that America is ready to rule itself as an independent country.

erosion to wear away.

fossil the hardened remains of animals preserved in the earth.

nickname a name that describes something special about a person or a place.

plateau a flat-topped mountain.

suspension bridge a bridge suspended from cables.

Web Sites

To learn more about Colorado, visit ABDO Publishing Company on the World Wide Web. Web site links about Colorado are featured on our Book Links page. These links are routinely monitored and updated to provide the most current information available.

www.abdopub.com

Index